First published in 2023 by Hungry Tomato Ltd.
F15, Old Bakery Studios, Blewetts Wharf,
Malpas Road, Truro, Cornwall, TR1 1QH, UK.

Thanks to our creative team:
Senior Editor: Anna Hussey
Senior Designer: Amy Harvey

Copyright © 2023 Hungry Tomato Ltd

Beetle Books in an imprint of Hungry Tomato.

ISBN: 978-1-915461-18-6

Printed and bound in China

Discover more at
www.hungrytomato.com
www.mybeetlebooks.com

PLANT

Written by Annabel Griffin
Illustrated by Tjarda Borsboom

Contents

Words in **BOLD** can be found in the glossary.

What Is a Plant?

Plants are living things that can be found almost everywhere on Earth! There are over 300,000 different types of plants on our planet. How many can you name?

Plants come in all sorts of shapes and sizes, but most of them have the same three parts: stem, roots, and leaves.

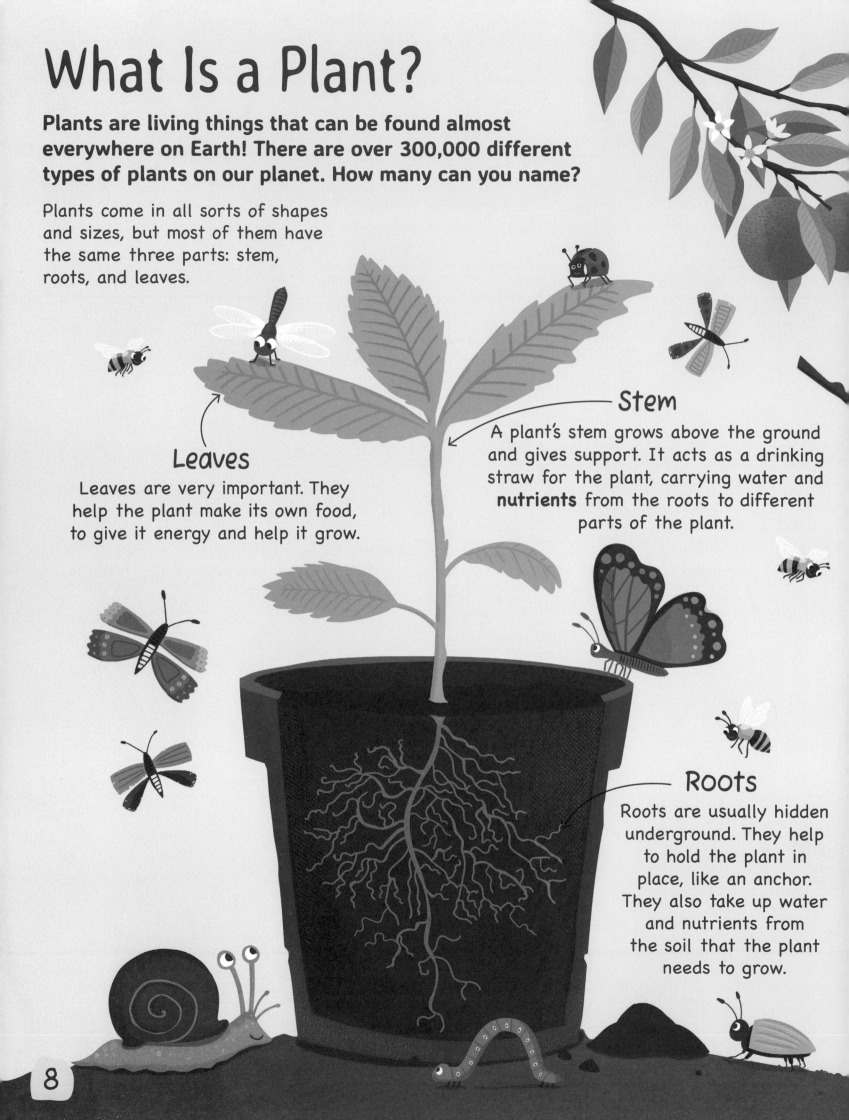

Stem

A plant's stem grows above the ground and gives support. It acts as a drinking straw for the plant, carrying water and **nutrients** from the roots to different parts of the plant.

Leaves

Leaves are very important. They help the plant make its own food, to give it energy and help it grow.

Roots

Roots are usually hidden underground. They help to hold the plant in place, like an anchor. They also take up water and nutrients from the soil that the plant needs to grow.

Blossom

Fruit

Berries

Some plants have other features, such as fruit, flowers, thorns, and branches.

Nuts

Flower

Petals

Thorns

Branches

Trunk

9

What Do Plants Need?

Plants can't grow without a few very important things: sunlight, air, water, and nutrients.

Sun
Plants take light from the sun and turn it into food, which gives them energy to grow.

Air and water
Without enough air and water, plants will quickly shrivel up and die.

Nutrients
The roots of a plant take up water and nutrients (food) from the soil.

Space
Some plants need space away from other plants, to avoid **competing** for nutrients in the soil.

By storing water, some plants survive in very hot places, like deserts.

Cactus

Some plants like water so much that they grow in ponds, lakes, rivers, or oceans.

RIBBIT

MOSS

Plants, like moss, grow on other things, such as tree trunks, branches, and rocks.

How Do Plants Grow?

Most plants grow from seeds. Even a gigantic tree starts its life as a tiny seed. How does it all begin?

Seeds

SUNFLOWER SEEDS

When a seed is planted and given water, it will begin to grow into a plant. This is called **germination**.

Shoot

1.
A root starts to grow out from the seed.

2.
A shoot grows up from the seed towards the soil's surface.

3.
The roots continue to grow as the shoot becomes a stem and starts to grow leaves.

Flower bud

4.
The plant grows bigger and stronger, creating more leaves and forming a flower bud.

5.
The plant reaches its full size and its flower opens.

Let's Grow a Seed
You will need:
- Sunflower seeds
- Large plant pot
- Peat-free potting compost

seeds

1. Read the seed packet to find the best time for planting.

2. Fill a large flowerpot with potting compost. Push a seed about ½ inch (1cm) down into the compost and cover it fully.

3. Place it in a sunny spot and water it regularly, so it doesn't dry out.

flower

13

How Do Bees Help Plants?

Bees are very helpful friends to plants. They carry **pollen** from one flower to another. This is called **pollination**. Plants need pollen from other flowers to make new seeds.

You look lovely

1.

Bees are attracted to a flower's bright petals and lovely scent.

Yummy nectar!

2.

Flowers contain nectar, a sweet liquid that bees collect to make honey.

3.
As a bee collects the nectar, it becomes covered in pollen, which is carried to the next flower it visits.

What Do Seeds Look Like?

Seeds come in lots of different shapes and sizes. Some seeds are nice to eat, and some are hidden inside fruit. Have you seen any of these seeds before?

Poppy

Once pollinated, a poppy will lose its petals and grow a **seedpod**, full of tiny black seeds.

The seedpod has holes, like a saltshaker, so seeds can blow out in the wind.

Sunflower

Sunflower seeds grow in the middle of the flower.

Wheat

Wheat seeds are used to make flour. They grow at the top of each stalk.

Apple
You've probably seen the seeds hidden inside an apple.

Strawberry
Strawberry seeds grow on the outside of each fruit.

Cherry
The hard stone inside a cherry is actually a seed.

Walnut
Nuts are also seeds! Most of them grow inside hard shells.

Corn
Did you know that corn kernels are seeds too?

17

How Do Plants Get Around?

Plants can't move around like animals, so they have to find other ways to spread their seeds.

OOPS

Seed splat
Some birds eat seeds and poop them out. Watch out!

Sticky seeds
Some seeds have little spikes or hooks that stick to an animal's fur, and get carried away to spread and grow.

Buried treasure
Squirrels bury seeds, storing them to eat in the winter. Forgotten seeds will remain buried and grow instead!

Dandelion seeds

Soaring seeds
Some seeds are blown away by the wind.

Maple seeds

Coconut

Lotus plant

Swimming seeds
Some plants, like coconuts and lotus plants, drop their seeds into water, to be carried away by the **current**.

Hazel

Seed explosion
Some seedpods explode or burst open, shooting their seeds away from the plant.

Squirting cucumber

Survival in the Desert

Deserts are hot, dry places, where there is very little rain. Some desert plants, such as cacti and agave, can store precious water in their stems or leaves; other plants must find different ways to get water.

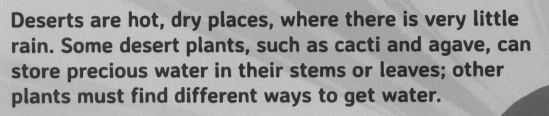

Please stop following me!

Tumbleweed

When a tumbleweed is fully grown, it separates from its roots and rolls away in the wind, spreading its seeds as it goes.

Water underground

Desert plants often grow very long roots that spread deep underground to find water.

Saguaro cactus
The saguaro cactus is the largest cactus in the USA.

Woodpeckers
Gila woodpeckers nest in holes that they make in the cactus with their beaks.

Night blooming
The cactus has flowers that stay open at night. They are pollinated by bats, who drink their nectar.

Owls
Little elf owls often move into nests that have been abandoned by the woodpeckers.

Perfect prickles
Cacti are covered in prickly spines, instead of leaves. They help the plants to collect water, stay cool in the heat, and protect them from animals that might try to eat them.

Beauty in the Rainforest

Tropical rainforests are home to thousands of different plants. Lots of different animals, including monkeys and birds, make their homes high up in the trees.

Lost in the forest

Scientists believe there may still be thousands more rainforest plants that haven't been discovered yet!

Tropical fruit

Tasty fruits like bananas and passion fruit grow in the rainforest.

Cacao pod

Orchids

Cacao trees grow large seedpods full of cacao beans, which are used to make yummy chocolate!

There are over 25,000 different types of orchid, and most of them grow in tropical rainforests.

Passion flower

Bromeliads

Passion flowers are some of the strangest and most beautiful flowers to grow in the rainforest. They also produce tasty passion fruit!

Bromeliads are plants that often grow high up on the branches of trees. Their leaves collect and hold rainwater, like a bucket. Poison dart frogs sometimes lay their eggs in the little pools of water.

Peaceful Pond Plants

Plants that grow in rivers, ponds, and lakes are called **aquatic** plants.

QUACK QUACK

Birds, like swans and ducks, make their nests among the reeds.

Plants like water lilies and reeds grow in marshy areas on the edges of ponds and lakes.

Some plants grow under the water and others float on the surface.

newt

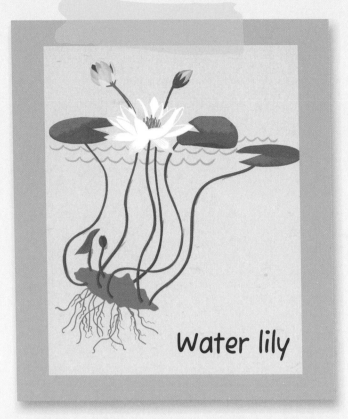

Water lily

Water lilies have wide, flat leaves that float on the surface of the water. Their roots reach down to the bottom of the pond.

Hornwort

Underwater plants like hornwort can provide safe hiding places for fish and newts.

Water hyacinth

These plants have swollen, spongy stems which are full of air to help them float. Their roots float freely in the water.

Cattails

Cattails, or bulrushes, are a type of reed that grows at the water's edge. They have sausage-like flowers.

Fragile Forests

Forests are large areas of land that are covered in trees. They are home to lots of different types of wildlife.

Tree houses
Some owls, foxes, squirrels, and other animals make their homes inside holes in trees.

Fun fungi
Mushrooms and toadstools can often be found growing in the forest. These are known as **fungi**.

Green planet
Different kinds of forests exist all over the world and cover about a third of the land on Earth!

Spring and summer

Trees can look very different depending on the season. In spring and summer, many trees grow lots of green leaves all over their branches.

Fall/autumn

Many trees go through a big change in fall/autumn. Their leaves change from green to red, yellow, orange, or brown. They also start to lose their leaves.

Winter

By winter, most tree branches are bare. Trees that lose their leaves in winter are called deciduous trees.

Some trees stay green all year round. They are called evergreen trees.

Adapting to the Arctic Tundra

The Arctic tundra is one of the hardest places for plants to grow in. It is very dark, cold, windy, and dry there.

Snow and ice covers the ground for up to 10 months of the year, and most of the soil remains frozen all year round!

There are no large trees in the tundra. Tundra plants are small and grow close to the ground. Most grow in the short summer, when the snow has melted.

In the winter, the temperature can fall to a bone-chilling -94°F (-70°C).

Many animals **hibernate,** or move to warmer areas, during the long, cold winters.

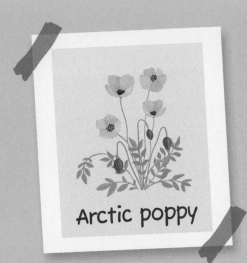

Arctic poppy

The flowers of the Arctic poppy move their faces towards the sun to soak up warmth and light.

Moss campion

Moss campion grows in cushion-like mounds. This helps it hold on to warmth and moisture.

Arctic cotton grass

Cotton grass has thin stems with fluffy cotton-ball tops. The fluffy balls contain tiny seeds, which are spread all over the tundra by the wind.

Bearberries

Bears love to snack on these berries.

Arctic bell heather

These little flowers have tiny leaves that overlap, like scales on a snake.

Arctic willow

The leaves of the Arctic willow are covered in long, fluffy hairs, to keep it warm.

Magnificent Meadows

A meadow is a large area of land that is mostly covered in amazing grasses and wonderful wildflowers.

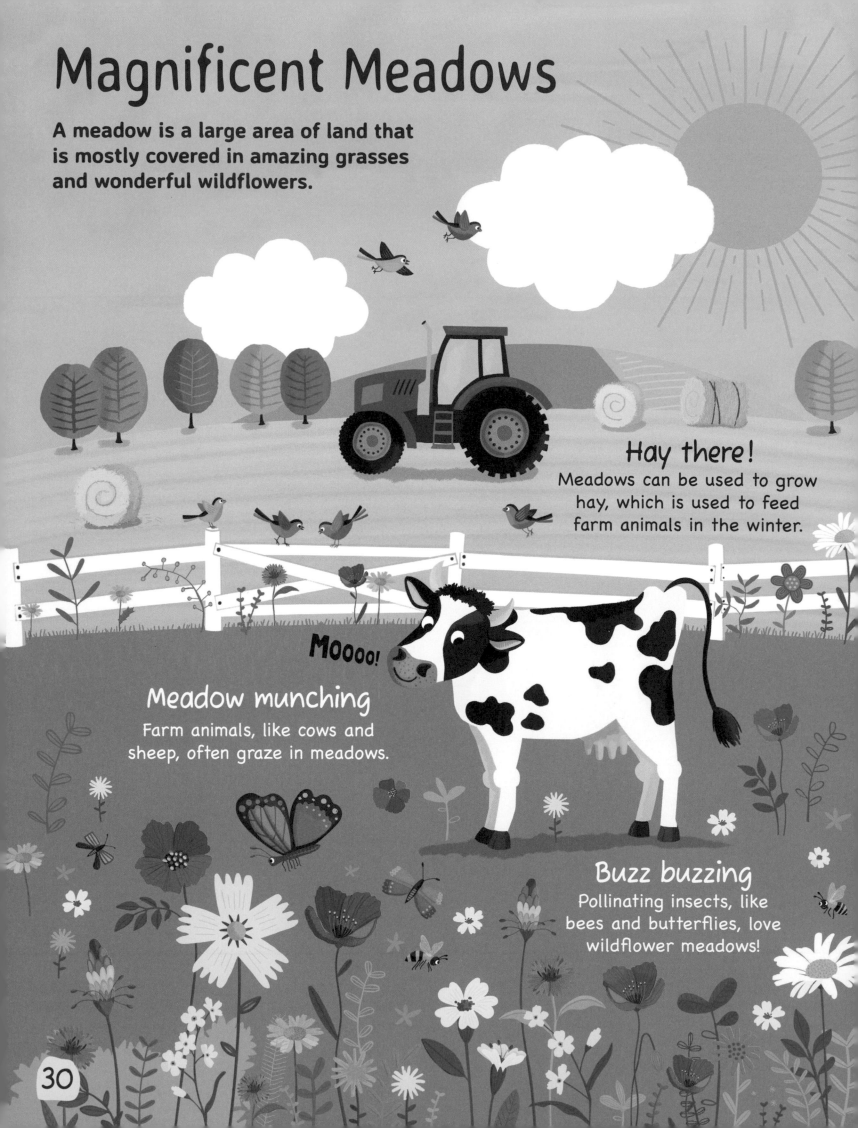

Hay there!

Meadows can be used to grow hay, which is used to feed farm animals in the winter.

MOooo!

Meadow munching

Farm animals, like cows and sheep, often graze in meadows.

Buzz buzzing

Pollinating insects, like bees and butterflies, love wildflower meadows!

Grasses

Wildflowers

About a quarter of plant life on Earth are grasses. They play an important role in keeping our planet healthy.

Wildflowers grow naturally in the wild. They are beautiful and attract wildlife, such as insects and birds.

Make Your Own Wildflower Seed Balls

Turn a patch in your yard/garden into a mini meadow.

You Will Need:

- Soil or peat-free compost
- Flour
- Packet of wildflower seeds
- Water

1. Mix together 3 ounces (85g) of compost, 1 ounce (28g) of flour, and a packet of seeds in a mixing bowl.

2. Add small amounts of water and mix with your hands until everything sticks together.

3. Roll the mixture into small balls and leave to dry in the sun.

4. Once dry, throw your seed balls into empty flowerbed spaces.

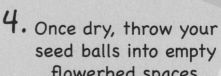

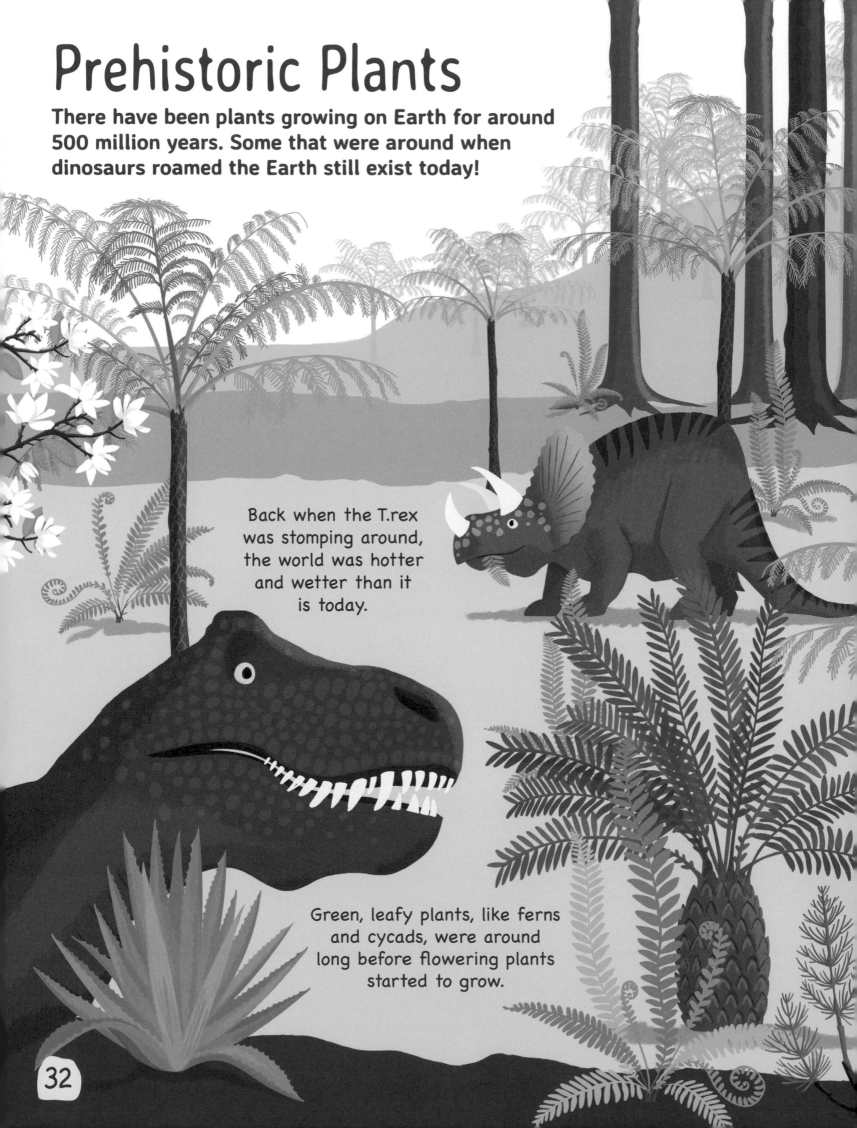

Prehistoric Plants

There have been plants growing on Earth for around 500 million years. Some that were around when dinosaurs roamed the Earth still exist today!

Back when the T.rex was stomping around, the world was hotter and wetter than it is today.

Green, leafy plants, like ferns and cycads, were around long before flowering plants started to grow.

Ginkgo trees

Ginkgo trees are **"living fossils"**. They have changed very little in 270 million years.

Horsetails

Horsetails existed millions of years ago. They were probably a tasty snack for plant-eating dinosaurs!

Tree fern

Tree ferns are a type of fern that have tree-like trunks. They grow very slowly, about 1 inch (2.5cm) per year.

Magnolia

Magnolias are one of the oldest known flowering plants. In the times before bees existed, flowers were pollinated by prehistoric beetles instead.

Cycad

Cycads and tree ferns aren't related, but look similar. Cycads produce cones full of seeds, whereas tree ferns create **spores.**

Hard fern

Ferns are one of the oldest groups of plants on the planet. If you went back 300 million years, you would find them!

Biggest Plants

The largest trees in the world stretch higher than some skyscrapers, even the Statue of Liberty!

380ft (116m)

325ft (99m)

305ft (93m)

300ft

200ft

100ft

Hyperion

General Sherman tree

World's largest tree

The General Sherman tree is the largest tree in the world, overall. It grows in California, USA, and is thought to be 2,200–2,700 years old.

World's tallest tree

The Hyperion redwood tree in California, USA, measures a mighty 380 feet (116m) in height. It's the tallest tree in the world!

El Árbol
del Tule

World's widest tree

El Árbol del Tule in Mexico is 46 feet (14m) wide. That's wider than the length of a bus!

46ft (14m)

40ft (12m)

World's biggest plant

The biggest plant in the world isn't a tree, it's a 4,500-year-old underwater seagrass meadow that has grown from just one **seedling** and spread!

Sea turtle

Dugong

The seagrass banks in Shark Bay, Australia, are the biggest in the world!

Smelliest Plants

Some plants smell good enough to eat, while others might put you off your food!

Callery pear

The Callery pear's blossoms may look pretty, but they smell like rotting fish. Ew!

Western skunk cabbage

As the name suggests, this plant smells like a stinky skunk!

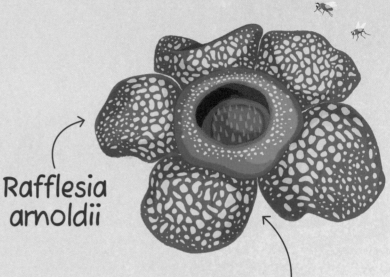

Rafflesia arnoldii

Corpse flowers

These two flowers have both been given the nickname "corpse flower", because they both smell like rotting flesh. The smell attracts flies and beetles. They are two of the biggest flowers in the world.

Hydnora africana

This strange-looking plant smells like poop, which is useful if you want to attract dung beetles.

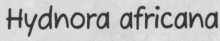

Titan arum

Cherry pie

This pretty purple flower smells like cherries and vanilla.

Caramel tree

This tree smells like caramel or cotton candy/candy floss.

Chocolate cosmos

These flowers smell like chocolate. Yum!

Popcorn cassia

This plant smells like buttered popcorn.

CHOCOLATE

Meat-eating Plants

Plants and insects are usually good friends, but some plants catch and eat bugs!

Venus flytrap

Venus flytraps eat almost any small bug! They have leaves that look like little mouths.

They quickly snap shut around the bug.

HELP!

They open wide and wait for a bug to land inside.

Flies, ants, beetles, grasshoppers, and spiders are all on the menu!

It takes 3–5 days to **digest** a bug. It may go months before its next meal.

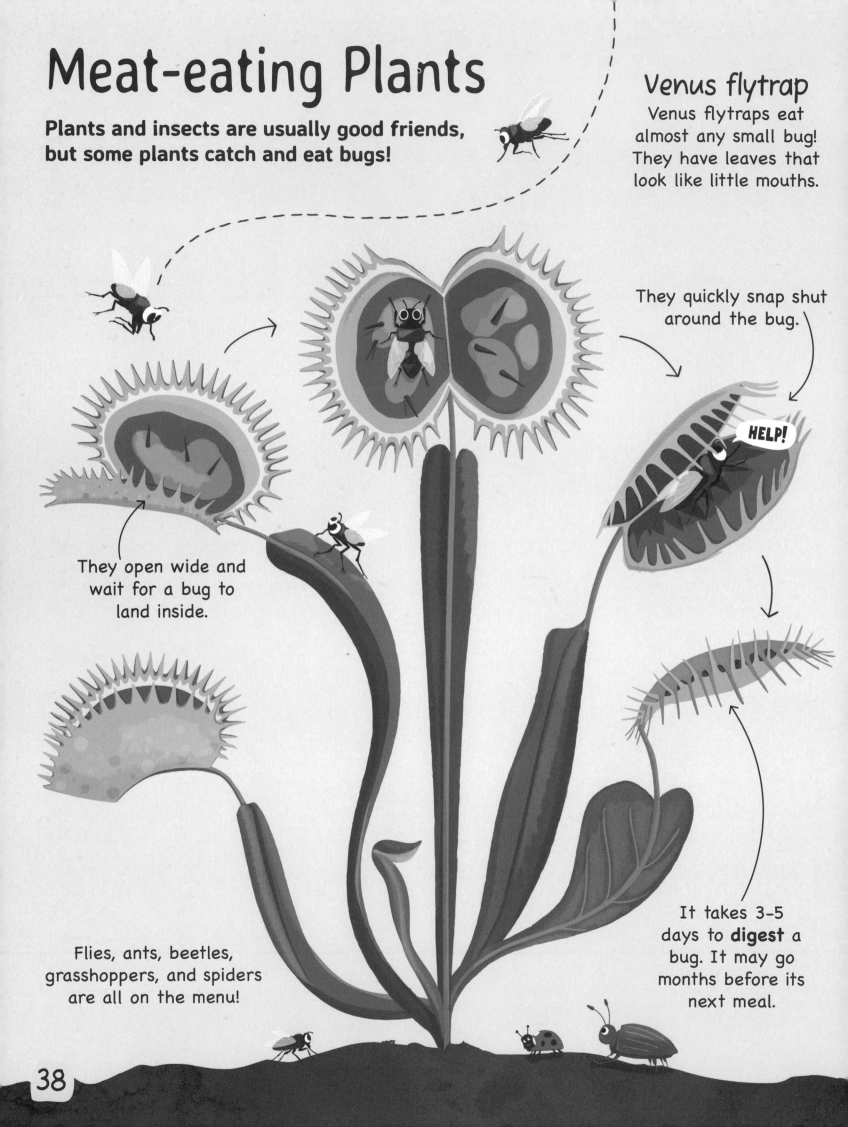

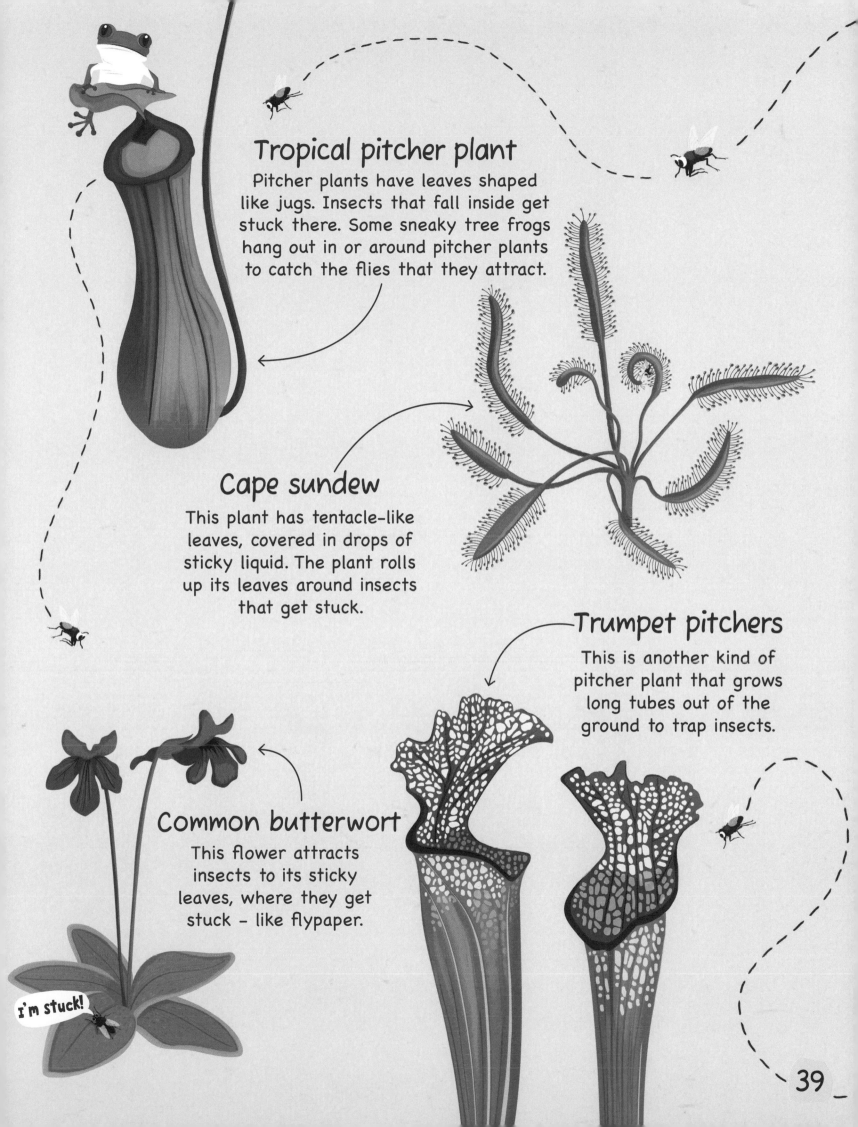

Tropical pitcher plant

Pitcher plants have leaves shaped like jugs. Insects that fall inside get stuck there. Some sneaky tree frogs hang out in or around pitcher plants to catch the flies that they attract.

Cape sundew

This plant has tentacle-like leaves, covered in drops of sticky liquid. The plant rolls up its leaves around insects that get stuck.

Trumpet pitchers

This is another kind of pitcher plant that grows long tubes out of the ground to trap insects.

Common butterwort

This flower attracts insects to its sticky leaves, where they get stuck – like flypaper.

I'm stuck!

39

Is It a Plant?

There are lots of weird and wonderful-looking plants. Some of them don't look like plants at all! Which disguise do you think is the best?

Hot lips
This rainforest plant has leaves that look like a pouty pair of lips.

Bee orchid
This look-alike flower even smells like a bee! It's trying to confuse real bees into pollinating it.

Lobster claws
A tropical plant with hanging flowers that look just like lobster pincers.

White egret orchid
An amazing flower that looks like a white bird in flight.

Egret

Bird of paradise
This beautiful flower is named after the bird of paradise because of its **elegant** shape.

Bird of paradise

Lithops
These strange-looking plants are often called "living stones" because they look similar to pebbles on the ground.

Mighty Moss

Moss is amazing! Mosses are small plants that grow in clumps. Sometimes, they spread out covering large areas, like grass. Mosses like damp, shady places, but will grow on almost anything, including trees, rocks and buildings.

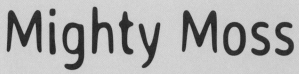

Mini forest

Moss is home to many **microscopic** creatures, including "water bears" (tardigrades).

Tallest moss

Not all mosses are small. Dawsonia superba is the tallest moss in the world, and can grow up to 24 inches (61cm) high.

Red sphagnum

Moss isn't always green.

Glowing moss

One moss, sometimes called goblin gold, seems to glow in dark places.

Dung moss

Some moss likes to grow out of animal poop! Yuck!

Let's Make a Moss Jar!

You will need:

- Moss
- Mixing bowl or large container
- Glass jar with lid
- Pebbles
- Soil
- Wood/twigs and stones to decorate
- Figurines/toys to decorate

If collecting moss outdoors, always ask permission, only take small amounts, and collect from areas where there is lots of moss.

1. Soak your moss in a bowl of water for 15 minutes.

2. Add a layer of pebbles to the bottom of your jar. Then add a layer of soil on top.

3. Arrange pieces of wood/twigs and stones.

4. Drain excess water from your moss, then place it on top of the soil, wood, and stones.

5. Add toys and put the lid on your jar. Place it somewhere indoors where it will get some sunlight, but not too much.

Plants at Home

You probably have lots of things made from plants all over your home.

Toiletries

Soap, shampoo, perfume, and make-up often contain parts of plants.

Outside

People with yards or gardens often grow plants for decoration, for food, or to help wildlife.

Heating

Wood is sometimes burned for heat.

Building
Wood from trees is often used to build parts of houses.

House plants
Having plants inside can make your home look great!

Clothing
Clothing and some fabrics, like cotton, can be made from plants.

Food
Fruits, vegetables, and cereals come from plants.

Books
Paper is made from wood. Without plants, books wouldn't exist!

Furniture
Chairs, tables, beds, storage, and other furniture is often made from wood.

Useful Plants

Some plants are really handy for turning into useful or beautiful things. Did you know that all of these things are made from plants?

Bamboo

Bamboo is used to make all sorts of things, from houses to toothbrushes. It is fast and easy to grow. Pandas also love it!

Rubber

When a rubber tree's **bark** is cut, it oozes a milky **sap**, called latex. People collect the latex and use it to make rubber. Rubber is used to make all kinds of things, such as balloons.

Perfume

Flowers that smell nice are often used to make perfumes, soaps, and other toiletries.

HAND SOAP

Fabrics

Some plants produce threads that can be spun into yarn, and used to make fabric.

Cotton

Cotton plants grow soft, white, fluffy balls of thread, which can be used to make cotton fabric.

Linen

Linen is another popular fabric. It's made from flax plants.

Dyes

Some plants can be used to dye fabrics.

Indigo

The leaves of the indigo plant are used to dye fabrics blue. Denim was traditionally dyed with indigo.

Henna

Leaves from this plant are dried and crushed into a powder to make henna. Henna can be used to dye fabrics, hair, and even skin for special occasions, such as weddings.

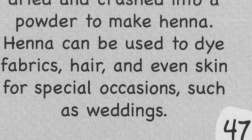

47

Good and Bad

People have been using plants to create medicines for centuries. Some plants have the power to both heal and harm, depending on how they are used.

Herbs to Use

Make Your Own

Cure With Herbs

?

Opium poppy

A milky liquid found in these poppies is used to make pain-relief medicine.

Foxgloves

Foxgloves are very poisonous plants, and can make people very sick! However, they also have something in them that can be used as medicine to help treat people with heart failure.

Yew

Yews are evergreen trees with red berries. Yew is poisonous, but its bark has been used in medicines to help treat cancer.

Rose periwinkle

This plant grows in Madagascar. It has been used to make medicine to help fight cancer.

Willow bark

The bark of a willow tree is a natural medicine. It's kind to our bodies and is often used to cure a nasty headache!

Aloe vera

Gel from inside the aloe vera plant can be used to help soothe burns, rashes, and dry skin.

St. John's wort

St. John's wort has a history of use in herbal medicine, dating back to ancient Greece.

Feeling Hungry?

Many different plants can be grown for food. Fruits and vegetables are an important part of a healthy diet.

Fruits

Fruits and berries usually grow on trees or bushes. They are often sweet and juicy.

Tomato

Leaves

The leaves of some plants, like lettuce, cabbages, and spinach, are great to munch on.

That leaf looks tasty!

Seeds and pods

Some tasty vegetables, like peas and sweetcorn, are really the seeds of their plant.

Fruit or veg?

Some foods that we call vegetables are actually the fruits of a plant, including pumpkins, cucumbers, and tomatoes.

Roots

Vegetables, such as carrots and beetroot, grow underground. They are the large tasty roots of the plant.

Bulbs

Onions and garlic are actually **bulbs.**

51

Herbs and Spices

Some plants are used to add extra seasoning or spice. Spices usually come from the seeds, fruit, roots, or bark of a plant, whereas herbs are from the leaves or stems.

Black pepper

Pepper is used to season lots of dishes. Peppercorns are tiny fruit that are usually dried and then crushed or ground into food.

Saffron

Saffron is the most expensive spice in the world. It comes from the flower of the saffron crocus.

Cinnamon

Cinnamon is a spice that comes from the bark of a cinnamon tree. It is often used in hot drinks and baking.

Chili (chilli) pepper

Both the fruit and its seeds can be used to add "heat" and spice to food.

Ginger

Ginger is a knobbly root that is used in a variety of dishes. It can be used fresh or dried.

Chives

Chives are related to onions and garlic. Their leaves have a similar taste, but aren't as strong.

Mint

Lots of things taste like mint. It can also be used as medicine, to settle stomach-ache!

Rosemary

Rosemary leaves can be used as a fresh or dried herb.

Chives

Rosemary

Basil

Basil leaves are used in lots of dishes around the world.

PESTO
alla genovese

Grow Your Own Chive Head

Chives can be used in salads and cooking.

You will need:

- Flowerpot
- Soil/peat-free compost
- Chive seeds
- Paints/pens
- Plastic eyes
- Glue
- Scissors

Chive Seeds

1. Decorate your pot using pens or paints, and plastic eyes.

2. Fill your pot with compost and plant your seeds, following the instructions on the seed packet.

3. Put your pot on a tray and place it on a sunny windowsill. Keep it well watered.

4. Once it is over 6 inches (15cm) tall, give your plant a haircut and use the cut chives in your cooking!

53

Planet Savers

Plants play a really important part in keeping our planet healthy.

Clean air

Plants take in **carbon dioxide** from the air and release **oxygen** through their leaves, which humans and other animals need to breathe.

CO_2

Too much carbon dioxide can lead to **global warming**! Planting more trees and plants will help to stop that happening.

Beautiful world

Plants help to make the world a beautiful place to be! Spending time in nature makes people happy.

Animal habitats

Trees and other plants are perfect **habitats** for animals. They provide food, shelter, and homes.

O^2

Clean water

Plants help to keep water clean by absorbing nutrients that could **pollute** it. Big plants, like trees, help to control the amount of rain that falls, reducing **droughts** and **flooding**.

Healthy soil

Fallen leaves and dead plants add nutrients back into the soil, keeping it healthy, so that other plants can grow.

Amazing Bugs

Did you spot the hidden creepy-crawlies on each page of this book? Creepy-crawlies are an important part of keeping plants healthy!

Buzzing bumblebees

Bees are one of the most important bugs. We rely on them to spread pollen, which helps flowers, fruits, and vegetables to grow.

Daring dragonflies

These prehistoric bugs have existed for over 300 million years! Dragonflies love ponds and wildflower meadows, where they hunt plant-eating bugs.

Wiggly worms

Worms are invertebrates, which means they don't have any bones! They wiggle through soil, eating dead plants and leaving behind nutrients for plants to soak up.

Beautiful butterflies

Butterflies have brightly patterned wings, making them the prettiest bug of all. Like bees, they drink nectar from flowers and pollinate yards, gardens, and meadows, helping new plants to grow.

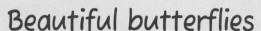

Pesky flies

It's true that some flies buzz around, eating plants, fruits, and vegetables. However, many flies actually help plants grow by pollinating them, just like bees do!

Brilliant beetles

Beetles can be all sorts of shapes and sizes. They are great because they hunt and eat bugs, like slugs and snails, that destroy plants.

Did You Know?

Plants are pretty amazing! Every living creature needs plants to survive, from eating them to living in them. The world wouldn't be the way it is today if we didn't have them. Did you know these amazing facts about plants?

70,000 plant species have been used for medicine!

MEDICINES

Plants that help

Home remedies

90% of food that humans eat comes from **30** plants!

One strawberry has around **200** seeds. That's a lot!

Have you ever wondered why an apple can float in water? It's because they are made up of **25%** air!

One tree, on average, can make up to **300,000** pencils!

Most pencils are made from cedar trees.

Bamboo is the fastest growing "wood" plant in the world. It grows **35** inches (89cm) every day!

A cluster of bananas on a tree has around **10-20** bananas on it.

A cluster is known as a "hand" and each banana is called a "finger"! They don't look the same as our hands and fingers, though!

Glossary

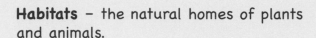

Aquatic – something that grows, lives, or spends a lot of time in water.

Bark – the tough outer layer of a woody plant stem or root, such as a tree trunk.

Bulbs – rounded parts of some plants that grow in the soil. They store food and shoots grow out of them.

Carbon dioxide – an invisible gas in the air that plants take in to make food and oxygen.

Competing – (verb) going against one another to gain or win something.

Current – the continuous movement of a body of water, such as a river or ocean.

Diet – food that you eat regularly.

Digest – (verb) to break down food into substances that can be absorbed and used by a body or plant.

Drought – a long period of dryness, usually caused by lack of rainfall.

Elegant – something that is graceful and stylish in appearance.

Flooding – when large amounts of water overflows into areas of land where it shouldn't be.

Fungi – (the plural of fungus). A group of living things, including mushrooms, molds/moulds and yeasts, that are neither plants nor animals. They reproduce using spores (see right) instead of seeds, and don't produce their own food, like plants.

Germination – the process when a seed begins to sprout roots and shoots.

Global warming – the rising temperature of the planet, which causes climate change.

Habitats – the natural homes of plants and animals.

Hibernate – (verb) to go into a deep sleep-like state for a long period during winter, when there is little food.

Living fossils – a type of plant or animal that has survived for a very long time with very little physical change, and is still around today.

Microscopic – something that is too small to be seen without the use of a microscope.

Nutrients – substances or ingredients that plants and animals need to live and grow.

Oxygen – an invisible gas in the air that plants produce, and people and animals need to breathe.

Pollen – a dusty powder made by some plants. It is used within pollination (see below) to produce new seeds.

Pollination – when pollen (see above) is moved from one plant to another – often by an insect – so the plants can make new seeds.

Pollute – (verb) to make dirty or harmful with waste, chemicals, or other substances.

Sap – a watery substance that comes out of a plant or tree.

Seedling - a young plant, grown from a seed.

Seedpod – a pouch or case produced by some plants to hold their seeds.

Spores – seed-like cells that some living things, including fungi (see left), mosses, and ferns, use to reproduce.

Index